❋ Let's Bake Bread ❋

❋ Hannah Lyons Johnson ❋

Let's Bake Bread

photographs by Daniel Dorn

Lothrop, Lee & Shepard Company ❋ New York

Also by Hannah Lyons Johnson
Hello, Small Sparrow

Johnson, Hannah Lyons.
  Let's bake bread.

  SUMMARY: Step-by-step instructions in the art of baking bread.
  1. Bread—Juvenile literature. 2. Baking—Juvenile literature. [1. Bread. 2. Baking] I. Title.
TX769.J63   641.815   72-9954
ISBN 0-688-41297-1
ISBN 0-688-51297-6 (lib. ed.)

2   3   4   5   77   76   75   74

❋ For My Mother and Father ❋

Special thanks to our enthusiastic bakers,
Tracy and Matthew Walter and Dylan Johnson

✳ Introduction ✳

Bread baking is a happy thing. All you need are a few good ingredients, some patience and a smile. The recipe in this book will make 2 loaves of simply scrumptious white bread.

It might be a good idea to read the book all the way through once, so you know ahead what you will be doing. Baking bread takes about 4 hours from start to finish, so you will need to plan on having enough time. (But you will not have to stay with your bread *all* that time.)

❋ Some Things You Will Need ❋

1. Large mixing bowl
2. Long-handled mixing spoon
3. Measuring cup
4. Measuring spoons
5. Flour sifter
6. Clean dish towel
7. Two loaf pans
8. Large breadboard
9. Long sharp knife
10. Rolling pin
11. Pot holders
12. Wire racks for cooling
13. Pan for scalding milk

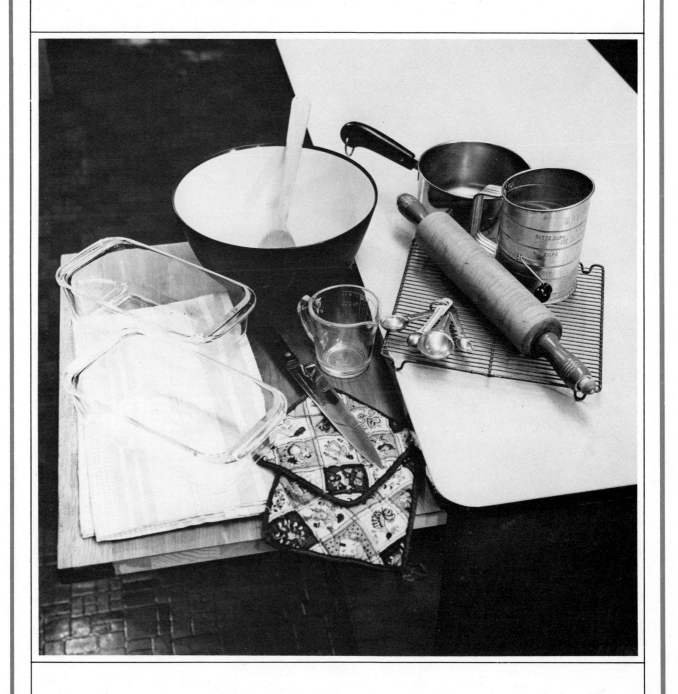

❋ What Goes Into Bread? ❋

1 package active dry yeast
¼ cup very warm water (105° - 115°)
2 cups scalded milk
¼ cup margarine or butter (that's ½ stick)
2 tablespoons honey
2 teaspoons salt
6 cups sifted unbleached white flour

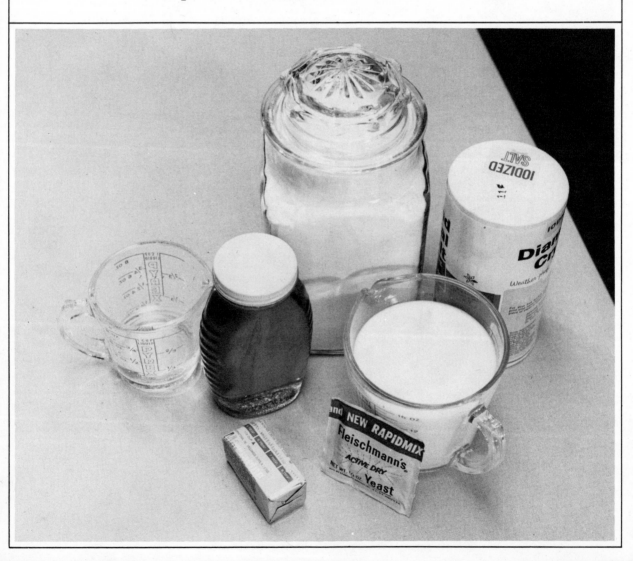

❋ Let's Begin ❋

First of all, wash your hands and fingernails. Then check to be sure all the utensils and other things are clean, too. If you want to wear an apron or smock, put it on and we'll begin.

❊ Step 1 / The Yeast ❊

Yeast is your living helper and partner. It looks like sandy grains, but is really tiny living plants that are dried and resting. By adding very warm water, you will wake them up. The yeast feasts on the honey in the bread dough and gives off a gas called carbon dioxide. This gas gets trapped in the dough and makes it rise up. Baking the bread kills the yeast.

Measure ¼ cup of water that feels very warm but not hot. (You may want to check the temperature of the water with a room or candy thermometer the first time.) Sprinkle the yeast into the water and let it sit for 5 minutes. Then stir it with a fork until all the yeast is dissolved.

❋ Step 2 / Starting the Dough ❋

To scald the milk, heat it until just before it starts to boil. Scalding the milk kills some enzymes in it which would keep the yeast from doing its work.

Pour the hot milk over the ¼ cup of margarine or butter, the 2 tablespoons of honey and the 2 teaspoons of salt that you have put in the large bowl. Stir until the margarine or butter, salt and honey are dissolved. Let the mixture cool until it is lukewarm (a drop of lukewarm liquid won't feel either hot or cold on your wrist).

✳ Step 3/Adding the Yeast ✳

Pour the yeast into the mixture and stir it so everything gets blended together well.

❋ Step 4 / Now the Flour ❋

Sift 3 cups of the unbleached flour into the mixture, and beat it well until it's very smooth.

❊ Step 5/You Have Dough ❊

Sift 3 more cups of the unbleached flour into the mixture and stir it very well until all the flour is completely blended in. This is hard stirring. It's nice to have someone help you here, to take turns stirring. The mixture is now bread dough.

❋ Step 6 / Kneading ❋

Clean out all the dough from the bowl and put it on a breadboard sprinkled with flour. Have extra flour handy to sprinkle on the dough so it won't stick to your hands or the board. (A damp dish towel under the board will keep it from slipping.)

To knead, push the dough down and away from you with the heel of your hand, and then fold it over toward you. Push it down and away again and fold it over again. Really lean and press on it.

Turn the dough around on the board as you knead so all sides get pushed and folded. Once in a while turn the whole piece of dough to its other side. Feel free to give the dough extra punches and slaps. It's great fun!

As you knead, sprinkle more flour on the dough a little at a time until the dough no longer sticks to you or the board.

Keep kneading for about 15 minutes. The dough will become very bouncy. When it feels very smooth and looks almost shiny, you have kneaded enough.

❄ Step 7/The Yeast Works Alone ❄

Pat the dough into a round shape. Grease the inside of your large bowl with margarine or butter. Place the dough into the bottom of the bowl and then turn it over so the top side is shiny with margarine from the bowl. This keeps it from drying out.

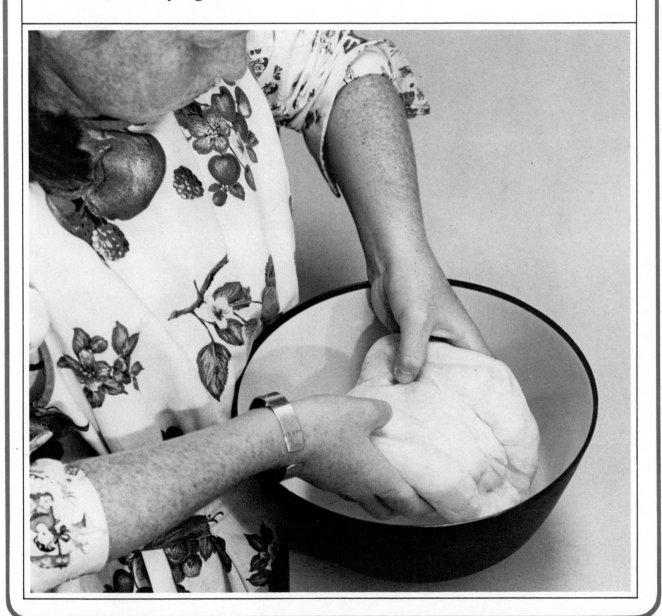

Yeast won't do its work where it's cold or drafty. A good place to put your dough to rise is in your cozy turned-off oven. If your oven doesn't have a pilot light to keep it warm, or is electric, put a pan of hot water on the rack under the dough each time it rises. This will keep the dough nice and warm.

Now cover the bowl lightly with the towel, close the oven door, and leave the dough alone for about 1½ hours until the dough doubles its size.

✻ Step 8 / Punching it Down ✻

The yeast needs some fresh air now. Turn the bowl over, let the dough drop onto the board and squeeze the gas out of it for about 2 minutes.

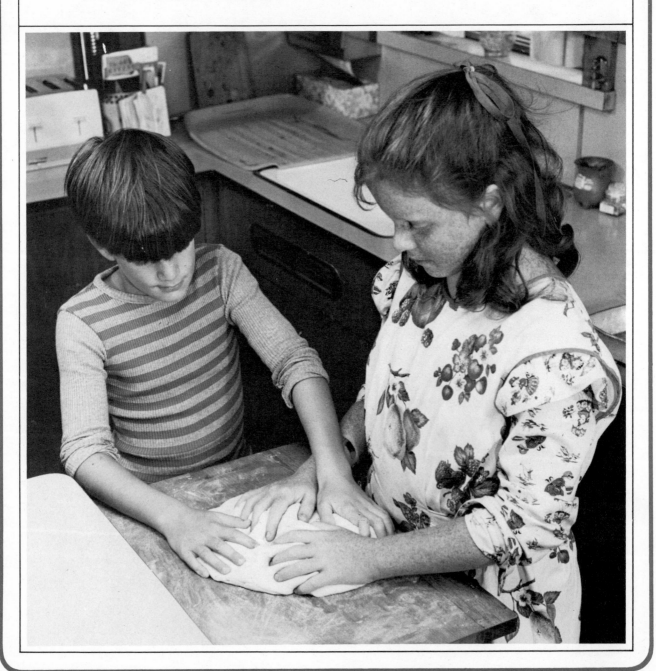

❋ Step 9/Forming the Loaves ❋

Pat the dough into a round shape. Cut the dough exactly in half with a knife.

On the board roll each half of the dough into an oblong shape that measures about 3 times wider than your loaf pan and 3 inches longer than your loaf pan. (If your pan is 5 inches wide and 9 inches long, your dough should be about 15 inches wide and 12 inches long, but it doesn't have to measure exactly.) The bouncy dough needs to be rolled hard to flatten it out. Rolling squeezes all the air bubbles out of the dough so your bread won't have big holes inside of it.

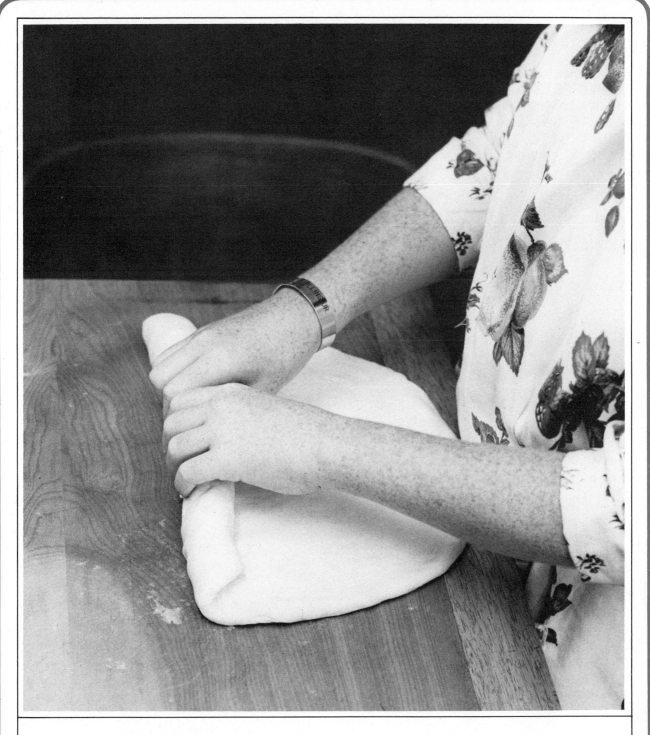

Starting at the narrow side, roll the dough up toward you. Be sure to roll as tightly as possible.

Now pinch the end edge of the roll into the roll. Then pinch the ends of the roll together and turn them up over the pinched edge.

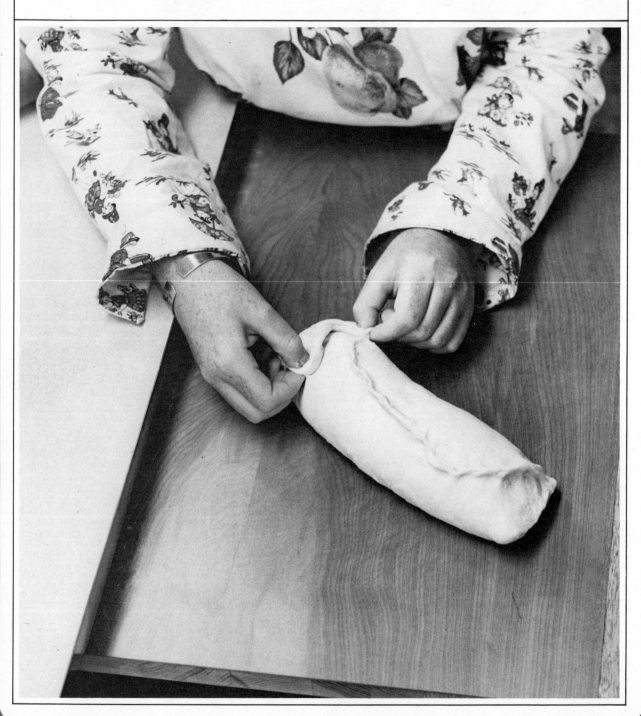

Place each roll into a loaf pan that you have greased with
margarine or butter. The seams and folded ends should
be on the bottoms of the pans. Make the loaves fit the pans
evenly by pressing the dough gently with your fingers.

Put the pans in the unheated oven, cover them and let the dough rise again for about 45 minutes or until it is a little higher than the sides of the pans.

✳ Step 10 / Baking ✳

Preheat your oven to 400° (this takes about 10 minutes), after you have put the covered pans in a place free from drafts.

Place the dough in the oven and bake it for about 30 minutes. Not all ovens heat or cook the same way. To be sure your bread is baking nicely, check it after it has been in the oven 25 minutes. It may need more or less baking time than 30 minutes.

After baking for a few minutes, the bread will send a delicious smell drifting through your house. Don't be surprised if your whole family follows their noses to the kitchen to wait for a taste of your bread.

When done, the bread is a golden brown color all over.

✳ Step 11 / Cooling It ✳

Turn off the oven. Using pot holders, take the pans out and let them cool a few minutes on a rack. Then turn the pans upside down and shake them gently, letting the bread slip softly onto the racks.

Cool the loaves right side up, away from drafts, for at least a half hour before you try to slice them. The cooler the loaf, the easier it is to slice.

This bread will have a slightly crunchy crust. If you want a softer crust, brush your loaves with melted margarine or butter while they are cooling.

❋ Step 12 / Storing the Bread ❋

Wait until the loaves are completely cool. Then put them in plastic bags and smooth the air out. Tie the ends of the bags tightly.

Home-baked bread will keep longer in the refrigerator. It freezes very well, too.

❋ Step 13 / Cleanup ❋

Wash and dry all the things you used and put them away for next time. You could even start your cleanup while the bread is rising.

❋ Some Afterthoughts ❋

After you get the hang of baking bread, you might want to try a new thing or two!

By doubling the recipe in this book, you can make 4 loaves at once, but stirring is doubly hard.

Try adding 1 cup of raisins to this recipe after you have sifted in the first 3 cups of flour.

A light whole wheat bread can be made by using 3 cups of whole wheat flour and 3 cups of unbleached white flour.

One cup of wheat germ added to the batter will make your bread even more nutritious.

By all means experiment with new ingredients. Perhaps you might even want to start a collection of bread recipes.

❁ A Gift of Love ❁

There is nothing more special than a gift you make your-self. Your own bread made with love and kindness will make your parents, grandparents, aunts or uncles, or any person dear to you very, very happy. And baking it is bound to make you happy, too.

641.8 Johnson, Hannah
JOH   Lyons

        Let's bake bread

DATE			